D1244944

COMFORT
AND JOY

COMFORT AND JOY

DAILY ADVENT DEVOTIONS

JULIE YARBROUGH

invite
PRESS

Plano, Texas

COMFORT AND JOY DAILY ADVENT DEVOTIONS

Copyright © 2022 by Julie Yarbrough All rights reserved.

Paperback ISBN 978-1-953495-43-3. eBook ISBN 978-1-953495-44-0

This book is printed on acid-free, elemental chlorine-free paper.

MANUFACTURED IN THE UNITED STATES OF AMERICA 09/30/22.

Cover photo by Julie Yarbrough is used with permission.

When the song of the angels is stilled,
when the star in the sky is gone,
when the kings and princes are home,
when the shepherds are back with their flock,
the work of Christmas begins:
to find the lost,
to heal the broken,
to feed the hungry,
to release the prisoner,
to rebuild the nations,
to bring peace among brothers,
to make music from the heart.[1]

For unto us a Child is born,
Unto us a Son is given;
And the government will be upon His shoulder.
And His name will be called
Wonderful, Counselor, Mighty God,
Everlasting Father, Prince of Peace.
Isaiah 9:6 NKJV

CONTENTS

QUEST FOR LOVE

QUEST FOR JOY

MEDITATIONS

God rest you merry, gentlemen,
Let nothing you dismay,
For Jesus Christ our Saviour
Was born upon this day,
To save us all from Satan's power
When we were gone astray:
O tidings of comfort and joy, comfort and joy,
O tidings of comfort and joy.

From God our heavenly Father
A blessed angel came,
And unto certain shepherds
Brought tidings of the same,
How that in Bethlehem was born
The Son of God by name:
O tidings of comfort and joy, comfort and joy,
O tidings of comfort and joy.

The shepherds at those tidings
Rejoiced much in mind,
And left their flocks a-feeding
In tempest, storm and wind,
And went to Bethlehem straightway,
This blessed Babe to find:
O tidings of comfort and joy, comfort and joy,
O tidings of comfort and joy.

But when to Bethlehem they came,
Whereat this Infant lay,
They found Him in a manger,

Where oxen feed on hay;
His mother Mary kneeling,
Unto the Lord did pray:
O tidings of comfort and joy, comfort and joy,
O tidings of comfort and joy.

Now to the Lord sing praises,
All you within this place,
And with true love and brotherhood
Each other now embrace;
This holy tide of Christmas
All other doth deface:

O tidings of comfort and joy, comfort and joy,
O tidings of comfort and joy.[2]

INTRODUCTION

If we forgive the gender implication in the title *God Rest You Merry, Gentlemen,* there is a message within its words that merits our deeper understanding. The historic meaning of the phrase 'God rest you merry' is 'may God grant you peace and happiness'. For many, Christmas is a time when we value superficial peace and happiness far more than authentic comfort and joy.

In this beloved English carol, the cadence of strong rhythmic verses is set off by a lyric refrain with words that reach into the heart of the celebration of Christ—tidings of comfort and joy. *God Rest You Merry, Gentlemen* tells a narrative Christmas story in five verses of music set to a traditional melody in a minor key. The carol concludes with a simple musical device known as the Picardy Third, a major chord at the end of a musical composition written in a minor key. The use of this device is both surprising and thrilling. The tension and dark overtones of the minor key are at once resolved with the triumphant flourish of the Picardy Third. The sudden shift from minor to major captures the transformative power of comfort and joy, the inspiration for the daily devotionals in this book.

Advent is the period in the Christian calendar that culminates in the celebration of the birth of Christ on the day we call Christmas. During this holy season of waiting, we meditate and prepare our hearts for the coming into the world of the promised Messiah.

For many, Advent is charged with vivid memories both of joyful celebrations and of seasons fraught with heartbreak and despair. From a place of dark shadows, many attempt to deflect the emotions of the season with a kind of spiritual indifference, reluctant to relive those painful experiences of the past engraved on the human heart.

Whether we approach the season of Advent with anticipation or with the overhang of emotional pain, at this affective time of the year there is within each of us a sense of deep longing for that which seems most elusive in the troubled world in which we live—light, comfort, love, and joy. These eternal qualities of God cannot be bought, borrowed, bartered, or appropriated from another.

Whatever our understanding or expectation of Christmas, Advent is a time to look within and listen for the voice of God. In a Christmas sermon from 1928, Dietrich Bonhoeffer observed, "The celebration of Advent is possible only to those who are troubled in soul, who know themselves to be poor and imperfect, and who look forward to something greater to come."[3]

And so at Advent we set ourselves the task of searching for something deeper, something richer that adds meaning and breadth to our spiritual understanding both of God and of ourselves, "His divine power has given us everything needed for life and godliness, through the knowledge of him who called us by his own glory and excellence . . . For this very reason, you must make every effort to support your faith with excellence, and excellence with knowledge, and knowledge with self-control, and self-control with endurance, and endurance with godliness, and godliness with mutual affection, and mutual affection with love" (2 Peter 1:3, 5-7).

Beyond mere searching and seeking, what if we were to transform our journey toward the manger from an exhausting daily slog through the traditions and rituals of the Christmas season into an active quest? What if we were to abandon the secular and focus our quest on thoughts and sights and sounds that spark our spiritual imagination, that inspire our heart and renew our unshakeable belief that God is alive in Christ in the world and in our life.

What is a quest? As translated from the medieval Latin, a quest is "a thing sought out, a question." Our Advent quest is the pursuit of that which heartens our spirit and floods our soul with the assurance of God present to us in Jesus Christ.

The questions of Advent are as many and varied as each human being, "Have you not known? Have you not heard? Has it not been told you from the beginning?" (Isaiah 40:21). "What does this mean?" (Acts 2:12). What is it that we are looking for? How do we know when we have found it and our quest is complete? What do we expect when we arrive at last at the manger? We will not know the answer until our quest leads us into the heart and very being of Christ. There we can do nothing more and nothing less than kneel at the manger in reverence, awe, and wonder.

In 1928, Senior Minister Dr. Umphrey Lee greeted the congregation of Highland Park United Methodist Church in Dallas, Texas with these seasonal thoughts:

> As we grow older, watching the passing of plans and men, feeling the touch of winter upon our heads and upon our hearts, we come to look forward to Christmas as the Festival of Beginning Again. The eternal youth of Christianity is in its insistence upon life, not upon life as mere duration here or hereafter, but upon that surging vitality of soul and spirit which is renewed hope, recovered love, belief in the future. All this the Christian means when we testify: "I believe in God." The essential faith begins with Bethlehem and the Child. He is forever that symbol of new life which is reborn in us today, a life that will not be bound by prejudice or meanness, that will not be held by our weakness nor by the gates of Death. May you all be happy at this Festival of Beginning Again.

Each year I look for a new Advent devotional book, confident that by reading it faithfully, there will be some overwhelming insight or inspiration that enlightens my personal experience of Christmas. Seldom is this the case. My heart longs to discover within the pages of an Advent devotional book some profound wisdom or bit of spiritual understanding that I have never considered before. I want to go deeper, to learn something I do not already know, something that ignites my soul with new passion, something that excites a deep yearning for a closer, more intimate relationship with God through Christ.

Within the pages of this Advent book, you will find a daily thought, a prayer suggestion, a study scripture, and an idea to consider for your Advent quest. Throughout the book there are meditations and excerpts from *Present Comfort: Meditations on Modern Loss and Grief* (Invite Press, 2021).

During these days of preparation and waiting, through the guidance of Scripture together we will consider in new ways the gifts of Light, Comfort, Love, and Joy. *Comfort and Joy* speaks to the heart of those who long for peace at a time when the challenges of the world seem overwhelming, to the heart of those who grieve and long for comfort, especially at Christmas, and to the heart of those who joy in the sacred celebration of Christ at Christmas. The hope is that as you read the devotional for each day, you will feel the presence of God in the living Christ. May the love of God hold you close at Christmas and always.

Quest for Light

Christ is coming, Christ has come,
let the world prepare a room.
God says: Light! and makes our day:
fear and chaos lose their say.
In our darkness shines our Sun;
God has made a date with man.

Christ has come, will come again,
parable of God and Man.
Lord of all our unborn days,
world renewing turn of phrase,
Word in season for all time,
godly reason, godly rhyme.

Let the earth make time and room
for the Man who is to come.
He, the center of our feast,
makes himself of all the least.
Stones and voices all proclaim:
There is bread in Bethlehem![4]

THE GLOW

At a museum gift shop one year, I selected some Christmas cards and asked a sales associate to explain the "buy one box and get half off the second box" promotional offer. As we discussed the transaction, I felt the woman sizing me up, trying to decide whether I was friend or foe because I dared to challenge the math of the deal. In fact, I was neither. I was just one more Christmas shopper trying to buy something on sale.

When we turned the corner in our conversation and got to a meeting of the minds about the price, we exchanged a small smile of mutual relief and finished the transaction. Before I turned to leave, she said rather shyly, "Your skin has such a nice glow."

I was surprised by the compliment. Perhaps she hoped I would share some skincare secret with her, or maybe she made the remark because I had used too much of a good thing that morning. As it happened, that very day I had purchased a new product that practically guaranteed a radiant glow. I was deeply touched by her personal outreach and quietly said "thank you" as I left. At the time, it seemed the better part of grace simply to acknowledge her kindness and be on my way.

As I returned to the city streets, I thought about the encounter and the real source of our glow. In the waning hours of the day, I watched people walking along, staring at smartphones that cast an eerie green glow on their faces. I saw others with the glow of lights and tinsel mirrored in their cold-kissed faces.

Our glow shines brightly when hope for the future overwhelms darkness in our lives. Our glow is brighter still when God's divine love illuminates our soul. The glow of Christmas shines in moments when our heart is strangely warmed by the certainty that God is present to us, that God is present with us.

In my brief retail experience with a lovely woman in the secular world of pre-Christmas shopping, I discovered yet again that our glow within comes only from the light of God. Christmas comes when we receive an unexpected blessing. Christmas comes when we are a blessing to others. The presence of God is the radiant glow that guides us through the season of celebration and lights our way at Christmas, "'I am the light of the world. Whoever follows me will never walk in darkness but will have the light of life'" (John 8:12).

Day 1

SILENT LIGHT

Now in that same region there were shepherds living in the fields, keeping watch over their flock by night. Then an angel of the Lord stood before them, and the glory of the Lord shone around them, and they were terrified. But the angel said to them, "Do not be afraid, for see, I am bringing you good news of great joy for all the people: to you is born this day in the city of David a Savior, who is the Messiah, the Lord. This will be a sign for you: you will find a child wrapped in bands of cloth and lying in a manger." And suddenly there was with the angel a multitude of the heavenly host, praising God and saying, "Glory to God in the highest heaven, and on earth peace among those whom he favors!"
Luke 2:8-14

Thought: Consider the darkness of a field at night suddenly interrupted by a light so brilliant it could be none other than the glory of the Lord. By its very nature, light is silent. Yet at Christmas, we superimpose the noise of our internal and external chaos upon the intrinsic purity of silent light. There has only ever been one event of noisy light in the history of humankind—when light, proclamation, and the music of a host of angels converged in an event of divine splendor to express the glory of God at the birth of Jesus Christ.

Prayer: God of silent light, as I enter into this season of preparation and waiting, may I live and move and have my being in the silence of your light. Amen.

Study Scripture: John 12:35-36

The Quest: How do you experience silent light in your life?

D a y 2

DARK LIGHT

The people who walked in darkness have seen a great light;
those who lived in a land of deep darkness—on them light has shined.
Isaiah 9:2

Thought: When we abide in darkness, it is almost unimaginable to contemplate the promise of light. Yet Scripture affirms the juxtaposition of darkness and light as the truth of prophecy made incarnate. We are told that in Christ, the darkness of the world will be overcome by a great light, once and for all time. We are told that a great light will shine on all those who have ever walked in darkness, and on those who live in a place of deep darkness. The dark, eternal night of human suffering is no challenge for the God of light. Christmas is about the light of the world, the embodied light of God's love in Christ shining into our darkness. As we prepare our hearts at Advent for the coming of Christ, let there be light.

Prayer: God of light, you are with me when I walk in deep darkness. Lift me out of the darkness of my life so that I may be a child of your light. Amen.

Study Scripture: 2 Corinthians 4:6

The Quest: What is your darkness? What is your light?

D a y 3

SHADOW LIGHT

How precious is your steadfast love, O God! All people
may take refuge in the shadow of your wings.
Psalm 36:7

Thought: Shadows are everywhere—around every corner, in every situation, especially at Advent and Christmas. Shadow is nothing more than darkness nuanced by light. Without light, there can be no shadow, only darkness, "If then the light in you is darkness, how great is that darkness!" (Matthew 6:23). In Christ there is no darkness, for hidden within every shadow is the light of God's love. Seek the light that casts no shadow in Christ Jesus the Lord. Seek the light that abides in the shadow of God's love.

Prayer: God, you are the light within every shadow. Find me where I am, bring me out of the shadows into the bright light of your love. Amen.

Study Scripture: Psalm 63:1-8

The Quest: Consider the shadow cast by wings. What image comes to mind when you consider God's steadfast love for you?

D a y 4

PEACE LIGHT

By the tender mercy of our God,
the dawn from on high will break upon us,
to give light to those who sit in darkness and in the shadow
of death, to guide our feet into the way of peace.
Luke 1:78-79 NRSV

Thought: The synchronicity of peace and light is evident at the dawn of each new day. Light creeps onto the horizon silently, peacefully, as the dark of night gives way to morning. At Christmas we cherish the familiar carol, "Silent night, holy night! All is calm, all is bright . . . Holy infant so tender and mild, sleep in heavenly peace."[5] Peace is the perfect calm of spiritual contentment. As the dawn from on high breaks into our life, we experience the light that guides our feet into the way of peace and assures us that we are loved by God. This is the heavenly peace of God in Christ Jesus.

Prayer: God of peace and light, in you I experience the living Christ. Open my heart to the dawn of your light. Amen.

Study Scripture: Psalm 85:8-13

The Quest: How do peace and light coexist in your life?

D a y   5

GRACE LIGHT

And the Word became flesh and lived among us, and we have seen his glory, the glory as of a father's only son, full of grace and truth.
John 1:14

Thought: Consider the many incarnations of light—candlelight, lamplight, sunlight, moonlight, the sparkling light of twinkling stars. When asked about the nature of light, a small child replied, "Light lets you see things." The gift of Jesus Christ to humankind is the quintessential expression of God's grace—God's love unearned, unmerited, and undeserved. Grace is pure gift. We have done nothing to be worthy of God's love. In Christ, God has given us everything we will ever need for a life of grace. One source affirms, "there is nothing in the world as tenacious and resolute as the grace of God."[6] At Christmas we celebrate the grace of God's light, "In your light we see light" (Psalm 36:9).

Prayer: God of grace, thank you for the power and glory of your light. May I shine the light of your grace into the hearts of others. Amen.

Study Scripture: John 1:16-18

The Quest: Where do grace and light intersect in your life?

Day 6

LOVE LIGHT

The Lord is God, and he has given us light.
Psalm 118:27

Thought: If you could give but one gift, the greatest would be love. God sent Christ into the world so that we might see in human form God's love in action, lived out by example. In Jesus, we behold the mystery of God incarnate, fully God and fully man. The love light of Christ reveals God's unconditional love for humankind—for you, and for God's children everywhere. No exceptions. This is the eternal light of love in Christ that can never be extinguished and will never die, "God's love was revealed among us in this way: God sent his only Son into the world so that we might live through him" (1 John 4:9).

Prayer: God of infinite love, you sent Christ into my brokenness so that I might know and see your love at work in the world. May I receive your love light and share it with others. Amen.

Study Scripture: Matthew 5:14-16

The Quest: In what way does the love light of God in Christ affect your heart and soul, especially at Christmas?

Day 7

EXUBERANT LIGHT

Light dawns for the righteous and joy for the upright in heart.
Psalm 97:11

Thought: There is nothing quite so mesmerizing as the light of a flickering flame that dances with intimations of joy. The exuberant light of a flame that wavers, steadies, then rights itself holds the promise both of physical warmth and spiritual blessing. Christmas is the celebration of a great, exuberant light that holds the promise of excitement, energy, and unlimited grace. Light is the reason for Christmas, the light of God's love shining into the darkness of humankind. Joy to the world.

Prayer: God of every light, I give you thanks for the exuberance of the light that sustains me at Christmas and always. May the Christ of light and love be present in my heart. Amen.

Study Scripture: Isaiah 60:19-20

The Quest: Search for the light in your life that never wavers and never grows dim. Pause, kneel, receive the gift of joy-filled, exuberant light.

Quest for Comfort

Away in a manger, no crib for a bed,
The little Lord Jesus laid down his sweet head.

The stars in the sky looked down where he lay,
The little Lord Jesus asleep in the hay.

The cattle are lowing, the baby awakes,
But little Lord Jesus no crying he makes.

I love Thee, Lord Jesus, look down from the sky
And stay by my cradle 'til morning is nigh.

Be near me, Lord Jesus, I ask Thee to stay
Close by me forever, and love me, I pray.

Bless all the dear children in thy tender care,
And take us to heaven, to live with Thee there.[7]

THE ORPHANS

The Dallas Arboretum is an urban oasis of natural and engineered beauty on the banks of a lake not far from downtown. This lovely place has been a refuge, especially since the death of my beloved husband. Before he died, we enjoyed going there together; after he died it became my grieving place "beside still waters."

On a crisp December afternoon three days before Christmas one year, I went to the arboretum to find a peaceful moment of "all is calm, all is bright." I left refreshed by the crisp beauty of a clear, cool day and the feeling of being far removed from the noise of the city and the season.

As I walked toward the exit, I happened to notice a display outside the gift shop. In what appeared to be a final effort to sell the remainder of the Christmas merchandise, there was a stand of long, decorated sticks intended as ornaments for a garden or yard.

They were pretty well picked over—the ones left at the end of the season seemed sad and pitiful. An imperfect Santa leaned against a sign that proclaimed "blessings." Several sagging soldiers were mixed in with a few lopsided angels. These were the decorations no one wanted. They were the unwanted, inanimate retail "orphans" left over from yet another season of intense commercialism. Their abandonment drew me in.

On the way home, I stopped by a megastore for a container to hold one last batch of Christmas cookies. Though the store was already winding down the push for Christmas, on the aisle with the last of the stocking candy and desperation gifts for last-minute shoppers I saw other orphans—plastic knickknacks in faded seasonal colors, slightly dented tins, and the last of the tired wrapping paper and ribbons.

Since that day, I have thought about orphans and our need for God's presence and comfort, especially at Christmas. There is surely nothing more heartbreaking than a child of any age without the love, affection, and protection of a caring adult, whether a natural parent, an adoptive parent, a foster parent, or someone who needs the two-way blessing that only a child can offer, "Give justice to the weak and the orphan; maintain the right of the lowly and the destitute. Rescue the weak and the needy" (Psalm 82:3-4). However orphaned we may feel at Christmas, God is present to comfort and uphold us—we are never alone, "For all who are led by the Spirit of God are children of God" (Romans 8:14).

There are spiritual orphans all around us who need an out-stretched hand of compassion, love, welcome, and inclusion, especially at Christmas. Perhaps we are orphaned by social isolation because we have little connection to friends or a place of community. Perhaps we are orphaned by circumstance if we are quarantined or restricted in our physical contact with others by a disability, a handicap, or a contagious disease. Perhaps we are orphaned by a rupture in our family that seems irreparable, at least for the time being. At church one year on Christmas Eve I sat next to a woman who was estranged from her husband and children. Tearfully, she poured out her heart because she felt so alone and abandoned. She was an orphan in need of comfort, love, and hope, especially on that holy night.

God is with us when we feel forgotten, lost, and lonely, at Christmas. There are no spiritual orphans beyond the presence and comfort of God, "I will never leave you or forsake you" (Hebrews 13:5).

D a y 8

PRESENT COMFORT

*In the beginning was the Word, and the Word was
with God, and the Word was God.*
John 1:1

Thought: As the living embodiment of God, Jesus is the Word that was with God from the beginning of time and who is forever present to us as God. In Christ we claim much more than the transient comfort of the world, for in Jesus we experience the real presence of God. Through Christ, we are assured that God loves us, that God cares about us, that God is present to us every moment of every day. God meets us wherever we are in our life with enduring comfort. Take heart. Through the living Word in Christ, God is present. Here and now.

Prayer: God of presence, God of all comfort, at this Advent time of waiting and preparation, may I receive your comfort in the certainty that you abide in me as the Word. Amen.

Study Scripture: John 1:1-5

The Quest: How do you access the presence of God to experience comfort through Christ?

D a y   9

TENDER COMFORT

As a mother comforts her child, so I will comfort
you; you shall be comforted in Jerusalem.
Isaiah 66:13

Thought: Is there anything more tender than soothing a fretful child to sleep with the music of a lullaby? If you have ever had a child or held a child or if you are grieving the death of an infant or a child, you know first-hand the almost insatiable need of a child for the tenderness of comfort, which is at the very heart of love. For from a heart of love we give comfort, and at the heart of love we find comfort. In moments of tender comfort, whether with an infant, a child, or an aging parent, we feel the sweet breath of God's perfect love. The tender comfort of God's perfect love in Christ is the best of all that is eternal.

Prayer: God of tender care, may your comfort sustain me through your love in Christ the Lord. Amen.

Study Scripture: Isaiah 40

The Quest: Consider the tender comfort of an infant, the meaning of "holy infant so tender and mild."

Day 10

MERCY COMFORT

Nevertheless, I am continually with you; you hold my right hand.
You guide me with your counsel,
and afterward you will receive me with honor.
Psalm 73:23-24

Thought: Love, mercy, and grace—the nature of God in Christ. Though these spiritual qualities are inextricably linked, mercy acknowledges our fundamental need for the divine grace expressed by the coming of Christ into the world, "Surely goodness and mercy shall follow me all the days of my life; and I shall dwell in the house of the Lord my whole life long" (Psalm 23:6). We experience the mercy of comfort in the "nevertheless" of God's continual presence to us in Christ. God holds our hand continually, God guides us with counsel, God comforts us through the gift of mercy in Jesus Christ.

Prayer: God of promise and presence, in your mercy comfort me with your care. Amen.

Study Scripture: Psalm 23

The Quest: What is the balance of mercy, comfort, and grace in your life?

Day 11

HEART COMFORT

You will increase my honor and comfort me once again.
Psalm 71:21

Thought: When we long for deep comfort, often we ask, "Where is God?" This is a quest and question of the heart. At Advent we wait for the birth of Christ, for the appearance of God. Yet waiting is counterintuitive to human nature, especially in the instant-gratification culture of the twenty-first century. We are experts at doing, and impatient when we must wait. Waiting is a discipline of the spirit. Waiting is about courage and strength, "Wait for the Lord; be strong, and let your heart take courage; wait for the Lord!" (Psalm 27:14). Jesus offers heart comfort in the assurance that God is present to us always, "And I will ask the Father, and he will give you another Comforter to be with you forever. This is the Spirit of truth, whom the world cannot receive because it neither sees him nor knows him. You know him because he abides with you, and he will be in you" (John 14:16). Our hearts rejoice in the comfort of God, present to us always in Christ Jesus the Lord, "Be glad in the Lord and rejoice, O righteous, and shout for joy, all you upright in heart" (Psalm 32:11)

Prayer: God of my heart, still my inmost being to receive your comfort. My heart overflows with gratitude that you comfort me again and again and again through the love of Christ. Amen.

Study Scripture: John 14

The Quest: How do you live into comfort with courage and strength? Consider the command, "Do not let your hearts be troubled, and do not let them be afraid" (John 14:27).

D a y 1 2

MIND COMFORT

I will call to mind the deeds of the Lord; I will remember your wonders
of old. I will meditate on all your work, and muse on your mighty deeds.
Your way, O God, is holy. What god is so great as our God? You are the God
who works wonders; you have displayed your might among the peoples.
Psalm 77:11-14

Thought: At Christmas, commercial promotions suggest we should strive for perfection in those things which really matter the least—adornment, festivities, and excess of every kind. When we right-size the importance of the things of this world at Christmas, there is space to be mindful and meditate on the one who is perfect, ". . . for you enlarge my understanding" (Psalm 119:32). There is space to consider the exponential power of comfort, "Praise be to the God and Father of our Lord Jesus Christ, the Father of compassion and the God of all comfort, who comforts us in all our troubles, so that we can comfort those in any trouble with the comfort we ourselves receive from God" (2 Corinthians 1:3-4 NIV). Through the perfect Christ, God enlightens our mind and comforts our heart, "Do not be conformed to this age, but be transformed by the renewing of the mind, so that you may discern what is the will of God—what is good and acceptable and perfect" (Romans 12:2). Think and reflect on the wonder of God in Christ Jesus.

Prayer: God of wonder works and mighty deeds, quiet my mind, comfort my heart. For your way, O God, is holy. Amen.

Study Scripture: Proverbs 16

The Quest: What is your understanding and experience of comfort? On the spectrum of spirit comfort do you offer sympathy, empathy, or compassion to others?

D a y   1 3

SPIRIT COMFORT

Comfort, O comfort my people, says your God.
Isaiah 40:1

Thought: Spirit comfort is the circular experience of receiving the gift of God in Christ and in turn giving the gifts of love and compassion to those in need of comfort. Sympathy is caring in the moment. Empathy is the ability to understand and share in the feelings of another. Compassion is about the kind of authentic personal experience that allows us to feel into the suffering of another. Spirit comfort is compassion in action, "Therefore, as God's chosen ones, holy and beloved, clothe yourselves with compassion, kindness, humility, meekness and patience" (Colossians 3:12). In God's gifts of love, comfort, and compassion in Christ we experience the soul and spirit of the living God.

Prayer: God of compassion and love, may I offer your comfort to others in the spirit of the living Christ. Amen.

Study Scripture: Colossians 3:14-17

The Quest: Where on the spectrum of spirit comfort do your abilities lie? Do you offer others sympathy, empathy, or compassion?

D a y   1 4

SOUL COMFORT

*For in hope we were saved. Now hope that is seen is not hope,
for who hopes for what one already sees? But if we hope for
what we do not see, we wait for it with patience.*
Romans 8:24

Thought: Soul comfort is about hope, "Why are you cast down, O my soul, and why are you disquieted within me? Hope in God, for I shall again praise him, my help and my God" (Psalm 42:11). Christmas happens when the miracle of God's love comforts us in Christ, who is the hope of the world, "But this I call to mind, and therefore I have hope: The steadfast love of the Lord never ceases, his mercies never come to an end; they are new every morning; great is your faithfulness" (Lamentations 3:21-23). God comforts us at Christmas and always. Our soul rejoices in the gift of hope through Christ Jesus the Lord.

Prayer: God of hope, may the anticipation of Christmas be for me about the coming of Christ, the source of all hope, the comfort of my soul. Amen.

Study Scripture: Romans 12

The Quest: What is the steady source of hope in your life?

QUEST FOR LOVE

Angels we have heard on high
Sweetly singing o'er the plains
And the mountains in reply
Echoing their joyous strains
Gloria in excelsis Deo!
Gloria in excelsis Deo!

Shepherds, why this jubilee?
Why your joyous strains prolong?
What the gladsome tidings be?
Which inspire your heavenly songs?
Gloria in excelsis Deo!
Gloria in excelsis Deo!

Come to Bethlehem and see
Him whose birth the angels sing;
Come, adore on bended knee,
Christ the Lord, the newborn King.
Gloria in excelsis Deo!
Gloria in excelsis Deo! [8]

God, Thou Art Love[9]

If I forget, yet God remembers.
If these hands of mine cease from their clinging.
Yet the hands divine hold me so firmly that I cannot fall.
And if sometimes I am too tired to call for Him to help me,
Then He reads the prayer unspoken in my heart and lifts my care.

I dare not fear since certainly I know that I am in God's keeping,
Shielded so, from all that else would harm,
And in the hour of stern temptation, strengthened by his power.
I tread no path in life to Him unknown;
I lift no burden, bear no pain, alone;
My soul a calm, sure hiding-place has found:
the everlasting arms my life surround.

God, Thou art love! I build my faith on that.
I know Thee who has kept my path.
And made light for me in the darkness,
Tempering sorrow so that it reached me like a solemn joy.
It were too strange that I should doubt Thy love.

THE ANGEL WORE
SNEAKERS

. . . not just any old work shoes, but hot pink sneakers with shiny silver racing stripes. This particular angel had bright yellow curly hair, the perfect complement to her sunny disposition. She was the flower lady responsible for seasonal arrangements in the large gothic dining room of an historic estate house. Her job was to arrange and care for the vibrant displays of fresh Christmas greenery and flowers that brightened a moody space with soaring cathedral ceilings.

As I toured the oversized rooms of the vast estate on Christmas Eve, I realized that my spirit was unwilling to settle for an entirely secular holiday celebration. My head and heart loudly insisted on a spiritual experience of Christmas far beyond mere candles and wreaths. I wanted nothing more than to hear the angels sing.

When I entered the dining room, the angel in sneakers smiled brightly and asked with a broad Southern accent, "How are you today, Hon?" She was the spirit of pure joy, the light amid the gloom, the sun that warmed my heart on a bleak midwinter day. Tears flooded my eyes, for at that very moment the massive pipe organ in the balcony began to play my favorite Christmas carol, "Angels We Have Heard on High." In that shining moment, the noise and tinsel of the world faded away. For a twinkling, my spirit stood in the sacred presence of God.

Sometimes a word or gesture of comfort and grace from a stranger is more powerful than the hollow echo of empty cheer, especially at

Christmas. When someone meets us at the right place at the right time with a word or silent embrace, we are enfolded in the love and presence of God. Whether or not we believe in angels, encounters with those whom God uses to minister to us when we least expect it heighten our awareness of God's grace at work in the world.

In truth, the bright pink sneakers were the last thing about this special angel that got my attention that day. It was her pure, gossamer spirit and tender kindness that stilled my soul and spoke God's love to me. And if this one angel could reach into my forlorn, needy heart on that dreary Christmas Eve, how much more is God present to us every minute of our lives, especially when our heart is sad, world-weary, and worn?

In her warm spirit, her caring outreach to others, her meticulous attention to the beauty of the flowers she tended, I saw the presence of God. My soul took flight, my spirit soared, "And suddenly there was with the angel a multitude of the heavenly host praising God, and saying, Glory to God in the highest, and on earth peace, good will toward men" (Luke 2:13-14 KJV).

Day 15

FORGIVING LOVE

*Be kind to one another, tenderhearted, forgiving one
another, as God in Christ has forgiven you.*
Ephesians 4:32

Thought: At the heart of forgiveness is love. As flawed human be-
ings, we are in constant need of the forgiveness of God. Jesus came into
the world as an expression of God's forgiving love. When we are forgiven, we are at once fully reconciled with God. When we forgive, we
bless the spirit of another with the same gift of love that we ourselves
receive from God. The grace of forgiveness keeps no record and has
no memory of the past. Forgiveness has the power to transcend every
hurt, every wrong, and every misdeed, because in forgiveness, there is
the divine love of God through Christ.

Prayer: God of grace and forgiving love, may I forgive others,
even as you continually forgive me in Christ. Amen.

Study Scripture: Luke 1:67-77

The Quest: When you examine your heart, what is unforgiven?
What is unforgiving? What would move you toward forgiveness?

Day 16

FORGIVEN LOVE

. . . just as the Lord has forgiven you, so you also must forgive.
Colossians 3:13

Thought: Whether we live with real or imagined guilt about some action or perceived failure, we are absolved once and for all time through the forgiveness of God in Christ. God asks nothing more and nothing less of us than that we acknowledge our need for forgiveness. Forgiveness requires no accompanying narrative, self-justification, or self-reproach. There are no caveats in forgiveness. When we ask, we are forgiven. At the heart of forgiveness we experience God's unconditional love, the gift to us of Emmanuel, God with us, "So we have known and believe the love that God has for us. God is love, and those who abide in love abide in God, and God abides in them" (1 John 4:16).

Prayer: God of forgiving and forgiven love, at this season of Advent, may I abide in the grace of your forgiveness offered in the name of Jesus Christ. Amen.

Study Scripture: 1 John 4

The Quest: If forgiving is a challenge, consider the practice and discipline of holy forgetfulness—forgetting to remember—as you forgive others and in turn receive forgiveness for yourself.

Day 17

GRATEFUL LOVE

*Praise the Lord! O give thanks to the Lord, for he is
good, for his steadfast love endures forever.*
Psalm 106:1

Thought: Grateful love inspires us to bless others with no expectation of reciprocity. Grateful love urges us to generosity of soul and spirit. Grateful love grows us in kindness. Grateful love is rooted in humility. Grateful love inspires our desire to serve others. Grateful love refines our heart. Grateful love is an expression of thanksgiving to God, "I will give thanks to the Lord with my whole heart; I will tell of all your wonderful deeds" (Psalm 9:1). Grateful love is a sacred responsibility that honors God's gift to us in Christ, "Come and behold him, born the King of angels. O come, let us adore Him, Christ the Lord!"[10]

Prayer: God of every blessing, may my love for you proclaim a grateful and grace-filled heart. Amen.

Study Scripture: Psalm 100

The Quest: How does gratitude shape the expression of your love for God and others?

D a y   1 8

HEALING LOVE

Then your light shall break forth like the dawn, and your healing shall spring up quickly; your vindicator shall go before you; the glory of the Lord shall be your rear guard.
Isaiah 58:8

Thought: Healing love is at the heart of Advent and Christmas. In these days of preparation for the coming of Christ, we turn inward and examine the state of our soul. We forgive, even as we seek forgiveness. We embrace the humility of gratitude, knowing that all we have, all we are, and all we will ever be, are gifts from God. We seek wholeness born of hope. We long for peace in consequence of faith. The love that heals our heart, our mind, our soul, and our spirit is a love more perfect than we have ever before known. In Christ we greet our vindicator, the One through whom the glory of God is revealed in the healing love of Jesus our Lord, "But for you who revere my name the sun of righteousness shall rise, with healing in its wings" (Malachi 4:2).

Prayer: God of healing grace, may your love make me whole at Christmas and always. Amen.

Study Scripture: Psalm 103

The Quest: What inhabits my life that is in need of the healing love of Christ?

D a y 1 9

RESTORING LOVE

Be restored; listen to my appeal; agree with one another; live in peace; and the God of love and peace will be with you.
2 Corinthians 13:11

Thought: Restoring love is a gift of God that confers the grace of peace. Restoration comes through intentional prayer. Restoration comes when we listen and hear God's voice as it speaks to our heart in answer to our prayers. Restoration comes through spiritual struggle and surrender to God, "And after you have suffered for a little while, the God of all grace, who has called you to his eternal glory in Christ, will himself restore, support, strengthen, and establish you" (1 Peter 5:10). God's love poured out to us through Christ has the power to revive our heart and restore our soul. We do not need to understand how or why this happens, but we know with certainty that God is at the core of every spiritual transaction of restoration. Through Christ, the grace of God restores us and makes us whole

Prayer: God of peace, quiet my heart so that I may receive the gift of your restoring love in Christ Jesus. Amen.

Study Scripture: 2 Corinthians 13

The Quest: What place of brokenness or woundedness in your heart is in need of God's restoring love?

D a y   2 0

REDEEMING LOVE

*You are indeed my rock and my fortress; for your name's sake lead me and
guide me, take me out of the net that is hidden for me, for you are my refuge.
Into your hand I commit my spirit; you have redeemed me, O Lord, faithful God.*
Psalm 31:3-5

Thought: Christmas is the revelation of God's plan to redeem the
world through the gift of a Savior in Jesus Christ, "With everlasting
love I will have compassion on you, says the Lord, your Redeemer"
(Isaiah 54:8). God sent his only son to transform the world through
the grace of redeeming love. We are redeemed through God's forgiveness to a life of love and hope. At this holy season, we express the con-
viction of our faith in every act that bears witness to God's redeeming
love in the person of Jesus the Christ. We express the certainty of our
faith when we proclaim victory over death through the living Christ.
We are redeemed through God's faithful love revealed to us in Emmanuel, God with us.

Prayer: God of refuge, I commit my spirit to you certain of your
love and faithfulness. Prepare my heart for the celebration of your redeeming love in Christ, the Savior of the world. Amen.

Study Scripture: Isaiah 43:1-4

The Quest: How do you experience the power and grace of redeeming love in your life?

D a y   2 1

PERFECT LOVE

Beloved, let us love one another, because love is from God;
everyone who loves is born of God and knows God.
1 John 4:7

Thought: Christmas is about new life. In the birth of Christ, the vitality of the human soul and spirit is wrapped in love and hope for the future. At the intersection of our own mortality with perfect love, we encounter the presence of God in the living Christ. The perfect love of God instructs us to "go on toward perfection" (Hebrews 6:1). We do this when we love one another, "you shall love your neighbor as yourself" (Leviticus 19:18). Because we are born of God, we know God. God lives in us. God lives through us. Thanks be to God for the perfect love incarnate in Jesus Christ.

Prayer: God of grace and glory, you came to earth in Christ to prove your perfect love for humankind. May I love others in the name of Emmanuel, God with us. Amen.

Study Scripture: 1 Corinthians 13

The Quest: In what way is God's love perfected in you when you love others as you love yourself?

QUEST FOR JOY

Joy to the world! the Lord is come;
Let Earth receive her King;
Let every heart prepare him room,
And heaven and nature sing,
And heaven and nature sing,
And heaven, and heaven, and nature sing.

Joy to the world! the Saviour reigns;
Let men their songs employ;
While fields and floods, rocks, hills, and plains
Repeat the sounding joy,
Repeat the sounding joy,
Repeat, repeat the sounding joy.

No more let sins and sorrows grow,
Nor thorns infest the ground;
He comes to make His blessings flow
Far as the curse is found,
Far as the curse is found,
Far as, far as, the curse is found.

He rules the world with truth and grace,
And makes the nations prove
The glories of His righteousness,
And wonders of His love,
And wonders of His love,
And wonders, wonders, of His love.[11]

I salute you. I am your friend and my love for you goes deep.
There is nothing I can give you which you have not got,
but there is much, very much, that, while I cannot give it, you can take.
No heaven can come to us unless our hearts find rest in today.
Take heaven!
No peace lies in the future which is not hidden in this
present little instant.
Take peace!
The gloom of the world is but a shadow.
Behind it, yet within our reach is joy.
There is a radiance and glory in the darkness could we but see—
and to see we have only to look.
I beseech you to look!
Life is so generous a giver, but we, judging its gifts by the covering, cast
them away as ugly, or heavy or hard.
Remove the covering and you will find beneath it a living splendor,
woven of love, by wisdom, with power.
Welcome it, grasp it, touch the angel's hand that brings it to you.
Everything we call a trial, a sorrow, or a duty, believe me,
that angel's hand is there, the gift is there,
and the wonder of an overshadowing presence.
Our joys, too, be not content with them as joys.
They, too, conceal diviner gifts.
Life is so full of meaning and purpose,
so full of beauty—beneath its covering—that you will find
earth but cloaks your heaven.
Courage, then, to claim it, that is all.
But courage you have, and the knowledge that we are
all pilgrims together,
wending through unknown country, home.

And so, at this time, I greet you.
Not quite as the world sends greetings, but with profound esteem and
with the prayer that for you now and forever, the day breaks, and the
shadows flee away.

—*Fra Giovanni Giocondo (1513)*[12]

D a y   2 2

TRANSACTIONAL JOY

So they went with haste and found Mary and Joseph and the child lying in the manger. When they saw this, they made known what had been told them about this child, and all who heard it were amazed at what the shepherds told them.
Luke 2:16-18

Thought: The shepherds felt that it was urgent for them to see whether the good news announced by the angel was really true. In the time it took for them to travel to Bethlehem, they experienced fear, disbelief, wonder, confusion, and a range of human emotions that prompted more questions than answers. How could this be true? Why them? Did they really see and hear angels? These were simple, yet courageous men whose hearts were filled with both apprehension and anticipation. For the shepherds, seeing the child Jesus, being in his presence was a holy experience of transactional joy. Like the shepherds, as we hasten to the manger on this Christmas Eve, may we touch, feel, hear, and smell the experience of birth and believe with joy that this newborn child is the gift of God's love, Christ Jesus the Lord.

Prayer: God of miracles, I rejoice this day in the birth of a Savior, your gift of love to the world. Amen.

Study Scripture: Isaiah 7:14

Meditation: Transactional Joy – page 55

The Quest: On this holy eve, pray that that you will discover again the true meaning of Christmas—God's love for you.

– 43 –

D a y   2 3

SACRED JOY

To you is born this day in the city of David a Savior, who is the Messiah, the Lord.
Luke 2:11

Thought: On this Christmas Day, the day on which we celebrate the birth of the Savior of the world, the Messiah, the Lord, may the gift of God's love reach into your heart with comfort and joy. May the communion of the saints and all those you love and hold dear encourage your heart through the grace of transcendent, eternal joy. In Emmanuel, God comes to us at Christmas to assure us that we are loved and beloved. Whatever your experience of joy this Christmas Day, take heart. Christ the Savior is born.

Prayer: O God of all salvation, on this Christmas Day I rejoice in the gift of your son who came to earth to show me your love. May I live each day in sacred joy. Amen.

Study Scripture: Matthew 1:18-25

The Quest: On this day of holy celebration experience the miracle of Christmas. Feel your heart strangely touched by joy.

In the bleak mid-winter, Frosty wind made moan, Earth stood hard
as iron, Water like a stone;
Snow had fallen, snow on snow,
Snow on snow,
In the bleak midwinter, Long ago.

Our God, Heaven cannot hold Him,
Nor earth sustain,
Heaven and earth shall flee away
When He comes to reign.
In the bleak mid-winter
A stable-place sufficed
The Lord God Almighty—Jesus Christ.

Enough for Him, whom cherubim Worship night and day,
A breastful of milk,
And a mangerful of hay;
Enough for Him, whom Angels
Fall down before,
The ox and ass and camel
Which adore.

Angels and archangels
May have gathered there, Cherubim and seraphim

Thronged the air;
But only His mother In her maiden bliss,
Worshipped the Beloved
With a kiss.

What can I give Him, Poor as I am?—
If I were a Shepherd,
I would bring a lamb; If I were a Wise Man,
I would do my part,—
Yet what I can I give Him,—
Give my heart.[13]

Day 24

TENTATIVE JOY

*But the angel said to them, "Do not be afraid; for see—I am
bringing you good news of great joy for all the people."*
Luke 2:10

Thought: In proclaiming the birth of Jesus to ordinary men—
shepherds in the field—the angel acknowledges our human fear. Fear
promotes disbelief. Fear nurtures unbelief. Fear makes us tentative
about believing good news, especially good news of great joy. Yet it
is in joy, not in fear, that we claim God's love in the person of Jesus
Christ—God in the flesh, God alive in the world. In Christ we receive
God's greatest gift to humankind, comfort and joy to the world.

Prayer: God who understands my fears, open my heart to hear
the voice of the angel and receive your good news of great joy. Amen.

Study Scripture: Luke 2:1-7

Meditation: Tentative Joy – page 57

The Quest: What fears limit you to tentative joy?

Day 25

FRAGILE JOY

*This will be a sign for you: you will find a child wrapped
in bands of cloth and lying in a manger.*
Luke 2:12

Thought: Joy comes from within. Joy is the balance of peace and hope deep within our heart. Joy may require a certain discipline of spirit when we encounter life's most daunting challenges. Joy is the outcome of love, even in the face of death. According to Henri Nouwen, "Joy is the experience of knowing that you are unconditionally loved and that nothing—sickness, failure, emotional distress, oppression, war, or even death—can take that love away."[14] Joy is the certainty that God is with us as a child wrapped in bands of cloth, lying in a manger. Stars and signs—fragile, beautiful joy.

Prayer: God of steadfast love, may all that separates my fragile spirit from the fulness of your joy be overcome through Christ. Amen.

Study Scripture: Luke 1:26-38

Meditation: Fragile Joy – page 60

The Quest: What signs, what angel voices proclaim God's love to you?

Day 26

HEARTFELT JOY

*The shepherds returned, glorifying and praising God for all
they had heard and seen, just as it had been told them.*
Luke 2:20

Thought: If we plumb the depths of love, we find joy. Joy has a dynamic, indescribable quality all its own. The overwhelming joy experienced by the shepherds transformed their lives forever. As they returned to their flocks in the hillside fields of Judea, they knew that they would never be the same again. Their hearts were filled with joy as they glorified and praised God for all that they had heard and seen. They needed no theological explanation or exposition of what they heard or saw, nor did they ask "why?". As the first evangelists, the shepherds proclaimed the birth of a Savoir with excitement and joy to everyone they knew and to everyone they saw along the way. Those who heard their story were amazed. Like the shepherds, in seeing we believe. In believing we behold the glory of God in Christ.

Prayer: God of promise and prophecy, accept the gratitude of my joy for your gift of love born to us as a Savior. Amen.

Study Scripture: Luke 2:25-35

Meditation: The Noise of Christmas – page 62

The Quest: What occasions your heartfelt joy at Christmas? How do you live into heartfelt joy throughout the year?

D a y   2 7

QUIET JOY

. . . and Mary treasured all these words and pondered them in her heart.
Luke 2:19

Thought: Mary was not only religious, but also spiritual. She was quiet, thoughtful, and introspective. The angel Gabriel came to her to proclaim that she alone had been chosen by God for a human experience with a divine purpose. With the obedience of a faithful servant, she acknowledged that out of all the women on earth, God had selected her to be the mother of the Savior of the world, "for the Mighty One has done great things for me, and holy is his name" (Luke 1:49). She accepted her appointed part in the divine order of creation despite whispers of condemnation, judgment, and denunciation. She treasured the words of the annunciation and meditated on all that had been told to her. With a loving, selfless, humble heart, Mary entered into an event of eternal magnitude, an event of quiet, everlasting joy, "For nothing will be impossible with God" (Luke 1:37).

Prayer: O God of quiet joy, I listen for your voice. Speak your words of calling to me. Amen.

Study Scripture: Luke 1:46-55

Meditation: Quiet Joy – page 64

The Quest: Amid the chaos of a secular season, where do you find quiet joy at Christmas?

Day 28

SUSTAINED JOY

In the time of King Herod, after Jesus was born in Bethlehem of Judea, magi from the east came to Jerusalem, asking, "Where is the child who has been born king of the Jews? For we observed his star in the east] and have come to pay him homage." When they had heard the king, they set out, and there, ahead of them, went the star that they had seen in the east, until it stopped over the place where the child was. When they saw that the star had stopped, they were overwhelmed with joy. On entering the house, they saw the child with Mary his mother, and they knelt down and paid him homage. Then, opening their treasure chests, they offered him gifts of gold, frankincense, and myrrh.
Matthew 2:1-2, 9-11

Thought: The magi journeyed to Jerusalem to inquire about the birthplace of Jesus, the newborn child destined to be king of the Jews. These wise men from the east had seen a star and were convinced that it would lead them to where the child was. After they had travelled about six miles from Jerusalem to Bethlehem, the star stopped. They knew that they were in the right place, that they had arrived. Scripture tells us that even before they went in, they were overwhelmed with joy. They knew that they were about to experience the presence of God. When they saw Jesus with his mother, they bowed down and worshipped him. They did not come empty-handed. They were prepared. They brought fine, costly gifts—gold, frankincense, and myrrh. When they left, they returned to their own country by another road. With them they took the gift of sustained joy, for they had seen the glory of God in Christ Jesus the Lord.

Prayer: God of breathtaking joy, sustain my heart in your love. May I celebrate the birth of Christ every day of my life. Amen.

Study Scripture: Matthew 2:1-6

Meditation: Regifting – page 66

The Quest: What have you experienced on your Advent quest that will sustain your joy throughout the year?

QUEST FOR JOY
MEDITATIONS

Transactional Joy

As I was returning to the airport on a rainy Sunday afternoon after speaking at a Christmas service of remembrance, I saw a drive-through restaurant and decided to get a cold drink before turning onto the highway for the fifty-mile drive. There was no car ahead of mine, so I placed my order and proceeded directly to the window.

The woman who greeted me was not a typical fast-food employee. She looked much older than she probably was. Perhaps she had done some hard living or been a victim of challenging circumstance in her life. Her mostly gray hair was tied back haphazardly to reveal a face with a story to tell, its chapters etched into the wrinkles and folds of her leathery skin.

Yet her charming, rather lopsided smile was radiant. It drew me in. Her warm, engaging spirit suggested that with every transaction and personal interaction, there was the possibility of a new friend. Her manner and outreach far exceeded any standard customer greeting in the company handbook. In that brief moment of enterprise—I gave her $1.81, she gave me a cold drink—there was an experience of transactional joy that touched me deeply. I left certain that for one shining instant I had been in the presence of an unlikely angel.

In John 16:20 (NIV) we read this intimation of joy, "Very truly I tell you, you will weep and mourn while the world rejoices. You will grieve, but your grief will turn to joy." The promise grows more exciting in verse 22, "Now is your time of grief, but I will see you again and you will rejoice, and no one will take away your joy." While both verses clearly acknowledge the reality of sorrow and grief, they overflow with hope and the promise of joy.

At Christmas, often there is a disconnect between superficial merrymaking and transactional joy. We may be surrounded by friends, family, and those we call family, yet we may be unable or unwilling to enter into the organized good cheer of a seasonal gathering. We ask, "What's wrong with me?" because we long for something more, something deeper, something richer than mere holiday festivity. Transactional joy cannot be experienced in emotional isolation. There are always two parties to any transaction.

One of my small Christmas traditions is to donate to the Salvation Army Red Kettle drive. For many years, there was a red kettle outside my local drugstore with an enthusiastic bell ringer soliciting donations. In recent years, the only place to donate has been at a local mall. Instead of a red kettle waiting to be stuffed with crumpled bills, there is a red tripod with a forlorn, dangling chain. Instead of a volunteer, there is a sign on how to donate by text. Though an electronic contribution lacks the human interaction of transactional joy, for those in need it makes no difference whether blessing originates in cyberspace or in a red kettle.

Christmas comes when our hearts are touched by joy. Christmas comes when someone—a friend, a relative, or a complete stranger—reaches out to us in love. Christmas comes when we reach out to someone else in love—a friend, a relative, or a complete stranger—with no expectation other than the potential for joy, their joy and ours. At the heart of transactional joy is the presence of God, the source of all joy. Within every transaction of soul and spirit there is the gift of love—Emmanuel, God with us.

TENTATIVE JOY

At this time of the year, most of us can recall a vignette of some kind that is part of our personal lore of the season. Some experiences we cherish and remember for a lifetime, others persist in memory, though in truth they may be better forgotten.

In the family photo album carefully assembled and curated by my father, there is a picture of me at age three sitting on Santa's lap. Back in the day, there were no mall Santas. You had to go to a department store for this particular Christmas experience. The best Santa was always at Sears, Roebuck and Company, because they had the largest selection of toys anywhere to be found. Their marketing strategy was to get kids into the store to touch, see, imagine, and dream.

Like most little girls there, I was dressed in my "Sunday best." In the photo I am wearing a white blouse and a gray flannel pleated skirt with shoulder straps, much like the one that Eloise wears in the eponymous books by Kay Thompson. Other than shiny patent leather shoes, my only accessory is a full plaster cast on my left arm—but that's another story.

Beyond the image of a small girl sitting on Santa's knee, the photo reflects the conflicted emotions of a child overwhelmed by a larger-than-life man in a red suit. In the picture I am leaning back to create the space and distance needed to process the experience—in essence, I am giving Santa the "stiff arm" with my good right arm. My body language clearly messages my reluctance to entrust a strange man with the desires of my heart, probably not much more than a doll of some kind and a peppermint stick.

At three years old, I was already a pragmatist. The photo tells the story of a small skeptic weighing the pros and cons of going all in with Santa. It captures both my serious reluctance and understandable fear of an overly jovial, unfamiliar man. Clearly, I was conflicted by the "should" of Santa joy and the reality of the unknown. Is there any wonder why so many pictures taken with Santa are of children awash in tears?

Pause for a moment to think about a group of shepherds at work in the hills of Judea near Bethlehem tending their flock of sheep on a starry night. Imagine their awe and wonder when an angel suddenly appears and tells them not to be afraid. Scripture tells us that they were terrified. Imagine how they received the "good news of great joy." Imagine, too, their shock and confusion over what had just happened. Did they blink their eyes in disbelief after the angels departed?

Yet one shepherd believed that God had revealed something extraordinary to them. Without a moment's hesitation, he said to the others, "Let's go to Bethlehem!" This man of great faith was eager, indeed excited to see the child announced to them as the long-awaited Messiah. There was nothing tentative or fearful about him. His work as a shepherd had taught him well that to waver for even a moment was to risk losing his flock. The shepherds dropped everything and went to Bethlehem with absolute faith in the power of God to transform humankind.

For many, the holiday season is about superficial pleasure and merriment rather than the pursuit of deep spiritual joy. Those who are grieving the death of a loved one may feel sad, tentative, or conflicted about entering into the festivities. We fear that if we participate, somehow our loved one will be set aside, lost, or forgotten within the celebration. Yet in truth, no occasion or holiday festivity has the power to diminish or deny the enduring love we share with one we love, "Love knows no limit to its endurance, no end to its trust, no fading of its hope; it can outlast anything. It is, in fact, the one thing that still stands when all else has fallen" (1 Corinthians 13:7-8 PHILLIPS).

Christmas is an opportunity to discover anew God's love—the love that holds us close, the love that defeats every fear, the love that understands a tentative heart, the love that overcomes the world. This is the love of Emmanuel, God, with us, at Christmas and always.

FRAGILE JOY

When life takes on new form and new shape, especially after death or the traumatic separation from a loved one, often we question our capacity for joy. At some point, most who grieve acknowledge that the one who is no longer present would want us to live a rich, joy-filled life.

Joy requires a certain single-minded resolve of spirit. We relearn joy slowly, imperceptibly as we release past resentments and put away our unfulfilled hopes and dreams of all that might have been. We may need to redevelop the muscle memory of our heart before we can again fully enter into the experience of joy. For a while, joy may feel fragile. We grow in faith when we yield our heart to whispers of love and memories that stir our heart to fragile joy.

Some obstinately resist joy. The apostle Thomas was both a pragmatist and a skeptic who had no use for secondhand joy. Only indisputable evidence could persuade the original "Doubting Thomas" to trust a sacred moment of incontrovertible joy. He needed proof before he could enter into joy.

> But Thomas (who was called the Twin), one of the twelve, was not with them when Jesus came. So the other disciples told him, "We have seen the Lord." But he said to them, "Unless I see the mark of the nails in his hands, and put my finger in the mark of the nails and my hand in his side, I will not believe."
>
> A week later his disciples were again in the house, and Thomas was with them. Although the doors were shut, Jesus came and stood among them and said, "Peace be with you." Then he said to Thomas,

"Put your finger here and see my hands. Reach out your hand and put it in my side. Do not doubt but believe." Thomas answered him, "My Lord and my God!" Jesus said to him, "Have you believed because you have seen me? Blessed are those who have not seen and yet have come to believe."

—John 20:24-29

When a baby is born, we experience the kind of fragile joy that is charged with hope and expectation. Though we know with certainty that life will not be perfect beyond the divine moment of birth, we do not reject the perfection of a baby because of possible adversity at some distant time in his or her life. Rather, with overflowing love and gratitude for new life, we enter wholeheartedly into the moment of fragile joy that teeters between celebration and the unknown future.

On a blustery fall day, I felt a kind of fragile joy as I watched the last leaves of autumn chatter across the road in a sudden gust of wind. Though there was no real reason for my surge of feeling, I knew that it was joy—joy to be alive, joy to see the beauty of nature in its fading glory, joy simply to be in the world.

At the epicenter of every joy is Christ the Lord, "for you have been my help, and in the shadow of your wings I sing for joy" (Psalm 63:7). There is nothing fragile in our joy when we sing and celebrate God with us in Emmanuel. Sing for joy, the Lord has come!

The Noise of Christmas

On a museum visit a few days before Christmas, there was an exhibit I especially wanted to see that was on display in a remote corner of the top floor. Perhaps the idea behind such a strategic location was to get visitors to hike through some of the less-frequented areas of the museum. Indeed, it was quite an adventure to find the room on the map and trek down the long, winding corridors. When I got there, I was alone. It seemed that I was the only person interested in blue and white porcelain on that particular December day.

It was blissfully silent, almost unnaturally quiet. As I stood admiring the artistry of each individual piece, I became aware of a noise, an insistent tap-tap-tapping headed in my direction. My first thought was, "Who wears rude shoes to a museum?" My concept of a museum as a place of relative quiet was challenged by the loud approach of someone who had just as much right to be there as I did.

Shame and self-reproach washed through my soul as I saw a young, visually impaired man making his way down the hall, assisted by the steady arm of an encouraging companion and the sure sight of his long cane. When our paths crossed, he made a U-turn and kept walking. Perhaps he sensed my presence, but clearly, he was focused on moving ahead.

I sat down for a moment to consider the noise so necessary for his connection to life. I wondered, too, what a blind man could see in a museum. Perhaps he was there to gain the confidence necessary for a life of self-determination and independence. While I was there to look at created beauty, he was there to learn how to navigate the world. Disturbed by my rush to judgment, I left deep in thought about the noise that constantly surrounds us and the spiritual blindness that easily convicts us.

A well-known quote is attributed to Helen Keller, who was both blind and deaf, "The only thing worse than being blind is having sight but no vision."[15] Gratefully, most of us will never know what it feels like to be blind and live in darkness or to be deaf and live in silence. In those moments when we feel spiritually blind, for a while we must grope our way through the darkness because we cannot see the true light of life. When our heart is transformed from darkness into light through the love of God incarnate in Christ, we see a clear vision for the rest of our lives.

Though we would like it to be otherwise, we cannot will whatever momentary pain there is in our life to be over just because it is Christmas. As the sounds of Advent urge us toward the manger, we may need to listen through the darkness, trust our heart, and follow the noise of the season, "Let me hear joy and gladness; let the bones that you have crushed rejoice" (Psalm 51:8).

Jesus was born into the noise of earthly life—the clip-clop of a weary donkey, the insistent sounds of hungry manger animals, the sighs of a mother in labor. Perhaps the birth of Christ was not such a "silent night" after all. If we do not pay attention to the noise, we may miss the experience of Christmas.

With the heavenly music of an entire chorus of angels and the brilliant light of a radiant star, God proclaims that a Savior is born to all the world. As we kneel to worship Christ the Lord, may the carol of our soul be the most beautiful noise of all as we see, hear, and receive the gift of Emmanuel, God with us.

QUIET JOY

Though my heart was broken with grief, somewhere deep within I knew that it was impossible to distance myself entirely from the festivities of the holiday season. There are no grief rules; we are allowed to participate. Slowly my pragmatic resistance to all things commercial thawed, and so I mixed it up with the crowds to see what the season was all about. I listened to the high energy of noise all around and watched for sights that awakened my spirit as reluctantly, yet inevitably I moved yet again toward Christmas.

On the sidewalk a solo trombonist played "O Come, O Come, Emmanuel" with off-key abandon. His honest spirit drew me in. I sensed my heart awakening to the message of the music. As I waited for a cab, I heard a street-corner rendition of "Angels We Have Heard on High." Suddenly I remembered that this is my favorite Christmas carol and felt a small smile of joy in my heart. The lights on Park Avenue shouted, "It's not too late; don't miss it!" There was urgency in their message of joy. At church on Sunday the sermon was on awakening. Its message seeped into my soul. The smell of incense aroused my senses with its mysterious, curling smoke, the symbol of prayer and hope.

I was humbled by the man on the street who had only one foot and silently asked for alms. His dignity fully intact, he seemed genuinely surprised when I honored his wordless entreaty and affirmed his human need with a small contribution toward his support. His dog was with him, perhaps to give him warmth. Or perhaps he was a faithful companion whose job was to help his master. The man had a friend; on that day he was less alone than I was.

The homeless man who sleeps most every night wedged into a side doorway at the church was not in his usual place. Yet his neatly packed worldly possessions stood on the sidewalk in silent testimony to his existence. It was my Christmas joy to tuck a bill into his bundle to acknowledge his life as a beloved child of God. Perhaps when he unrolled his bed in search of warmth and protection from another freezing night on the street, he found my small offering and knew that someone cared. In quiet joy may we be to others the hands and heart of Emmanuel, God with us.

REGIFTING

Giving something that we have received to someone else is known as *regifting*. This practice has been around for a long time but has become more acceptable in recent years. The urge to recycle our stuff is driven by a desire to rid ourselves of those things we do not want or need and will never use. We think that our castoffs might be used or enjoyed by someone else, so we pass them along as gifts. According to one survey, more than half of all adults agree that regifting is not objectionable if done with consideration and respect.

Etiquette experts generally agree on a few fundamental guidelines for regifting:

- Whatever the gift, someone has made the effort to give it. Before regifting, the giver should be sincerely thanked for his or her thoughtfulness.
- To qualify for regifting, the gift/merchandise must be in perfect condition, in its original packaging, with the instructions.
- The regifted item must be something the recipient needs or would like to have.
- The gift is not something that is one-of-a-kind, handmade, or personalized.
- Never regift something to the original giver.
- Never regift something to someone who might know the original giver.

- Remember that an unwanted gift might be a welcome donation to a charitable organization.

Those in the world who offer compassion and consolation to others regift their own emotions. Each expression of comfort comes from the heart and life experience of another, "This is my comfort in my distress, that your promise gives me life" (Psalm 119:50). When we receive the gift of comfort, we regift to others the comfort we ourselves have received from God,

> "For who has known the mind of the Lord?
>   Or who has been his counselor?"
> "Or who has given a gift to him, to receive a gift in return?"
> For from him and through him and to him are all things.
>   To him be the glory forever. Amen.
>   —Romans 11:34-36

God created us to love, "you shall love the Lord your God with all your heart, and with all your soul, and with all your mind" (Mark 12:30). We regift God's love for us and our love for God through the One who is "the way, the truth, and the life" (John 14:6). Spiritual regifting is circular, "Every good gift, every perfect gift, comes from above" (James 1:17 CEB). In regifting our gifts and graces to others, we experience the exponential power of Emmanuel, God with us. In Christ we receive the gift of love. In Christ we give the gift of love. Let us live in sustained joy as we love one another, "Just as I have loved you, you also should love one another" (John 13:34).

NOTES

1. Thurman, Howard, "The Work of Christmas." In *The Moods of Christmas & Other Celebrations,* 23. Richmond, IN: Friends United Press, 1985.

2. "God Rest You Merry, Gentlemen," *Carols for Choirs 5* (Oxford, United Kingdom: Oxford University Press, 2011), 56.

3. Dietrich Bonhoeffer, Dietrich Bonhoeffer's Christmas Sermons, trans. and ed. Edwin Robinson (Grand Rapids, MI: Zondervan, 2005), 21.

4. "Christ is Coming," Words by Fred Kaan, Copyright © 1975 Music by John Ness Beck, Copyright © 1975 (Carol Stream, IL: Hope Publishing Company, 1975).

5. "Silent Night, Holy Night," Words by Joseph Mohr, 1818, Music by Franz Gruber, 1818.

6. Farrell, Leighton. *Cries from the Cross* (Nashville: Abingdon Press, 1993) 24.

7. "Away in a Manger," Words by Anonymous, 1882, Music "Cradle Song" by William J. Kirkpatrick, "Mueller" by James R. Murray.

8. "Angels We Have Heard on High," Words - traditional French carol, Music - "Gloria" arr. Edward Shippen Barnes.

9. Robert Browning. *Paracelsus, Part V, "Paracelsus Attains"* from *The Poetical Works of Robert Browning, Vol. II* (London: Smith, Elder & Co, 1888), 142.

10. "O Come, All Ye Faithful," Words by John Francis Wade, 1751, Melody "Adeste Fideles" by John Francis Wade.

11. "Joy to the World," Words by Isaac Watts, 1719, Melody "Antioch" by George Frideric Handel.

12. Fra Giovanni Giocondo, from a letter written to Countess Allagia Aldobrandeschi on Christmas Eve, 1513, https://gratefulness.org/resource/joy-fra-giovanni-peace/ (accessed June 20, 2022).

13. Christina Rossetti. *A Christmas Carol. Scribner's Monthly: An Illustrated Magazine for the People*, January, 1872.

14. Henri Nouwen. *Here and Now: Living in the Spirit* (New York: The Crossroad Publishing Company, 1994), 28.

15. https://www.goodreads.com/quotes/6497288-the-only-thing-worse-than-being-blind-is-having-sight, accessed November 24, 2020.